By Adryan Moorefield
Conceived By Adryan Moorefield & TJ Perry
Illustrated By Naira Tangamyan

Hey There Little Black Boy

59 Affirmations To Help You Learn Your Feelings

AuthorHouse™
1663 Liberty Drive
Bloomington, IN 47403
www.authorhouse.com
Phone: 833-262-8899

Because of the dynamic nature of the Internet, any web addresses or links contained in this book may have changed since
publication and may no longer be valid. The views expressed in this work are solely those of the author and do not necessarily
reflect the views of the publisher, and the publisher hereby disclaims any responsibility for them.

Any people depicted in stock imagery provided by Getty Images are models,
and such images are being used for illustrative purposes only.
Certain stock imagery © Getty Images.

This book is printed on acid-free paper.

ISBN: 978-1-6655-3851-0 (sc)
978-1-6655-3852-7 (e)

Library of Congress Control Number: 2021919116

Print information available on the last page.

Published by AuthorHouse 10/12/2021

authorHOUSE®

How to Read This Book

This book is a guide to help you learn your feelings.
Whenever you feel a certain emotion, go to that section in this book.
Take a deep breath and pick a page.
Pick a sentence on the page and let that sink in. Lather, rinse, and repeat as often as you need to.
Use this book throughout the day whenever you feel overwhelmed by your emotions.
Before long, you will be equipped with the tools you need
to be a confident, well rounded, centered human being.

Appearance

Hey there little black boy,
love the skin you're in.
You are wrapped in kisses from the sun.
That glow will always win!

Hey there
little black boy,
your hair is beautiful
and strong.
It holds stories
from your ancestors.
Those tales are
never wrong!

Hey there little black boy, your shape is one of a kind.
Be healthy, live strong, have fun,
and laugh. What counts
is in your mind!

Hey there little black boy,
you're perfect just the way you are.
There's lots of people in
this world, but you are a special star.

Hey there
little black boy,
that reflection
you see is light.
Don't be afraid to
let it shine,
for yours is
really bright!

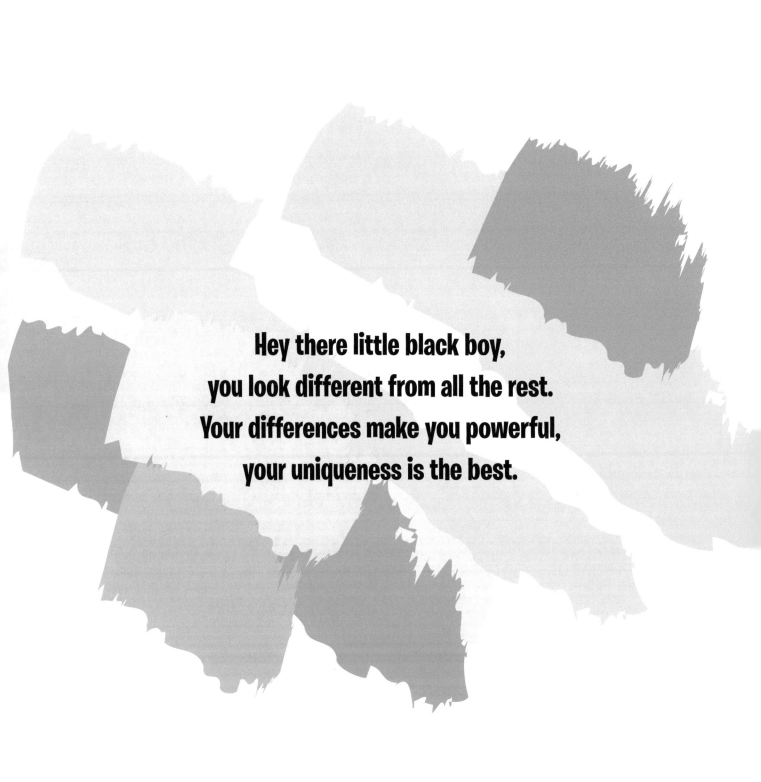

Hey there little black boy,
you look different from all the rest.
Your differences make you powerful,
your uniqueness is the best.

Hey there
little black boy,
your eyes are a
gorgeous shade.
They carry treasure
no one else knows,
your eyes are
wondrously made.

Hey there little black boy,
your lips are the perfect size.
They help you speak with authority,
from them will come no lies!

Hey there little black boy, your teeth are
just right! Your smile
can brighten any
room, just brush to
keep them white.

Hey there little black boy,
you are beautiful, yes indeed.
You are a gift given to
the world. Your gift is what we need!

Happy

Hey there little black boy, your smile is beautiful
and bright! It shines as strong as
one thousand suns.
It can light up any night!

Hey there little black boy,
you're feeling really good today.
Use that feeling, be kind and helpful,
your generosity goes a long way.

Hey there little black boy,
I've got a challenge for you.
Do something nice for someone else today,
then they'll be happy too!

Hey there little black boy, it feels so good
to play. Your laughter is contagious.
You will liven any day!

Hey there little black boy,
find joy in any place.
That power will cover your entire
being, it will keep a smile on your face.

Hey there little black boy,
go on and explore.
Your passions will propel you,
they can open any door.

Hey there
little black boy,
I watch you
sing and dance.
Your energy is
enchanting.
You've put me
in a trance.

Hey there little black boy,
I want to make a deal.
Be kind to others, don't pick and choose.
Care about how they feel.

Hey there
little black boy,
go ahead and
touch the sky.
No dream is
impossible.
No mountain
is too high!

Hey there little black boy,
you're not some
regular old thing. You descend from
royalty! Remember
you are a KING!

Sad

Hey there little black boy,
I see you're sad today! It's ok to feel
the way you feel,
something better could be
coming your way.

Hey there
little black boy,
your tears
are really wet.
It's ok to cry,
or talk things out,
you'll soon
feel better yet!

Hey there little black boy, your feelings really matter.
Don't let anyone tell you
otherwise, ignore
all that chatter!

Hey there little black boy,
you seem to be in pain.
That feeling will eventually disappear.
You'll soon feel good again.

Hey there little black boy, you won't always be the best.
Don't let the ranks define
you, there isn't any test!

Hey there little black boy,
sometimes things will be lost.
Memories are priceless,
they don't have any cost.

Hey there little black boy,
goodbyes can cause some strife.
Honor the time you
had together, that
growth is a way of life.

Hey there little black boy, you are a special
cup of tea. Not everyone
will like it but
that leaves more room
just for me!

Hey there little black boy,
things just aren't going your way.
Everyone has bad luck sometimes,
tomorrow's another day.

Hey there
little black boy,
friendships come and go.
Just give it time,
you'll find your tribe,
these friends
are Best in Show!

Angry

Hey there little black boy,
I see you're really mad.
Take a moment, think things through,
I'm sure things aren't that bad!

Hey there little black boy, someone was really mean.
It doesn't feel good to not
be heard, all you want
is to be seen!

Hey there little black boy,
be careful with what you say.
Words have meaning and
are strong too, you might regret it someday!

Hey there little black boy, you're throwing a big fit!
There are better ways to
communicate, but
first you have to quit!

Hey there little black boy,
it's hard when you don't agree.
Everyone has different
thoughts, you must accept this to be free.

Hey there little black boy, respect you
do deserve. Don't let others
put you down
but calm that raging nerve!

Hey there little black boy,
your patience is running thin.
Take a step back and breathe real deep.
The right words will help you win.

Hey there
little black boy,
your head is fuming
with steam.
You'll have the
urge to act it out,
find a pillow
instead and scream!

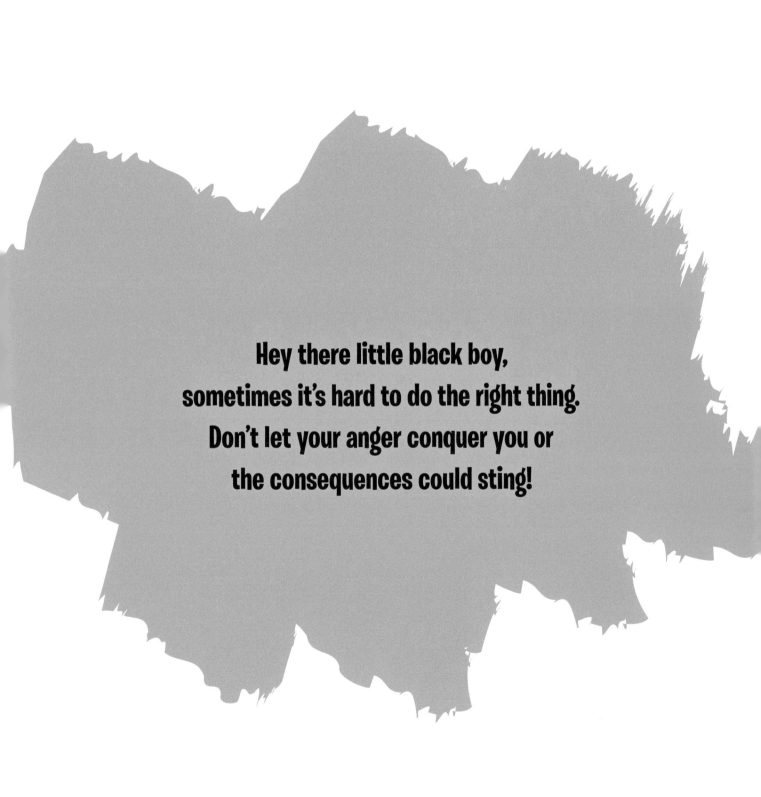

Hey there little black boy,
sometimes it's hard to do the right thing.
Don't let your anger conquer you or
the consequences could sting!

Hey there
little black boy,
life isn't always fair.
As frustrating as
that fact may be,
there's goodness
in the air.

Scared

Hey there little black boy,
you're shaking in your bones.
Everyone is afraid
of something.
I promise you're not alone!

Hey there little black boy, it's ok to cry.
That mountain might look real big,
you can climb it if you try!

Hey there little black boy,
you're stronger than you know.
The first step is always
the hardest, all you have to do is go!

Hey there little black boy, that job looks really tough.
Just give it your best, that's
all I ask, remember
you are enough!

Hey there little black boy,
did something frighten you?
Look your fear straight in
the face and tell that fear to move!

Hey there
little black boy,
the unknown
can be scary.
Take a leap of faith,
you've got this now.
There's no need
to stay wary.

Hey there little black boy, you can do it if you try.
The thought of failing can be
tough. Just spread
your wings and fly!

Hey there little black boy,
your fear can be a key.
It tells you when you should be careful,
that voice can help you see.

Hey there little black boy,
when fear looks you in the face,
sometimes there's strength in numbers.
All you need's a warm embrace.

Hey there
little black boy,
you won't
always be afraid.
With just a
little courage,
your fear will
start to fade.

Embarrassed

Hey there little black boy,
it seems you made a mistake.
Bloopers happen,
nobody's perfect.
If we were,
we'd all be fake!

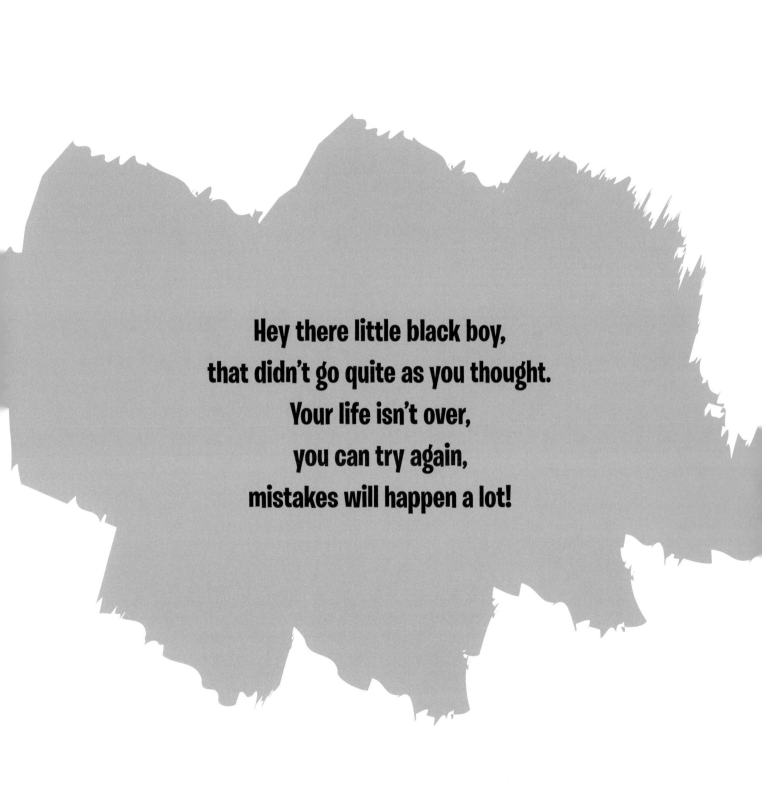

Hey there little black boy,
that didn't go quite as you thought.
Your life isn't over,
you can try again,
mistakes will happen a lot!

Hey there little black boy,
put that feeling
up on a shelf. Say,
"Hello, how are you?
I am human!
Don't be so hard
on yourself!"

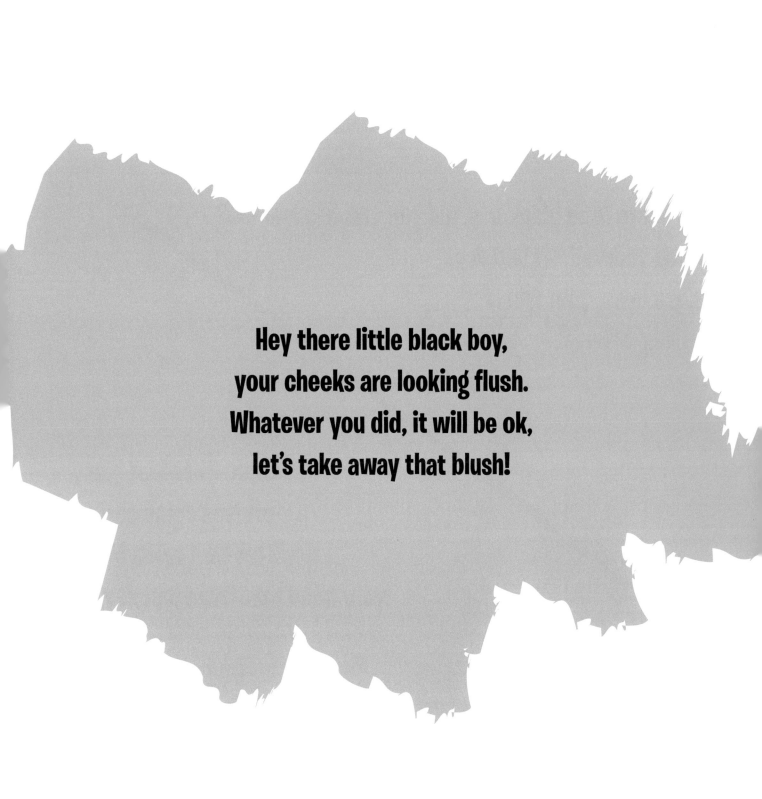

Hey there little black boy,
your cheeks are looking flush.
Whatever you did, it will be ok,
let's take away that blush!

Hey there little black boy, did you just trip and fall?
Brush yourself off and dry
those eyes, your win is
waiting afterall.

Hey there little black boy,
bruises come and go.
Don't let that voice inside
your head take over, just say no!

Hey there little black boy,
there's no need to feel ashamed.
Everyone has their moments,
for that you can't be blamed.

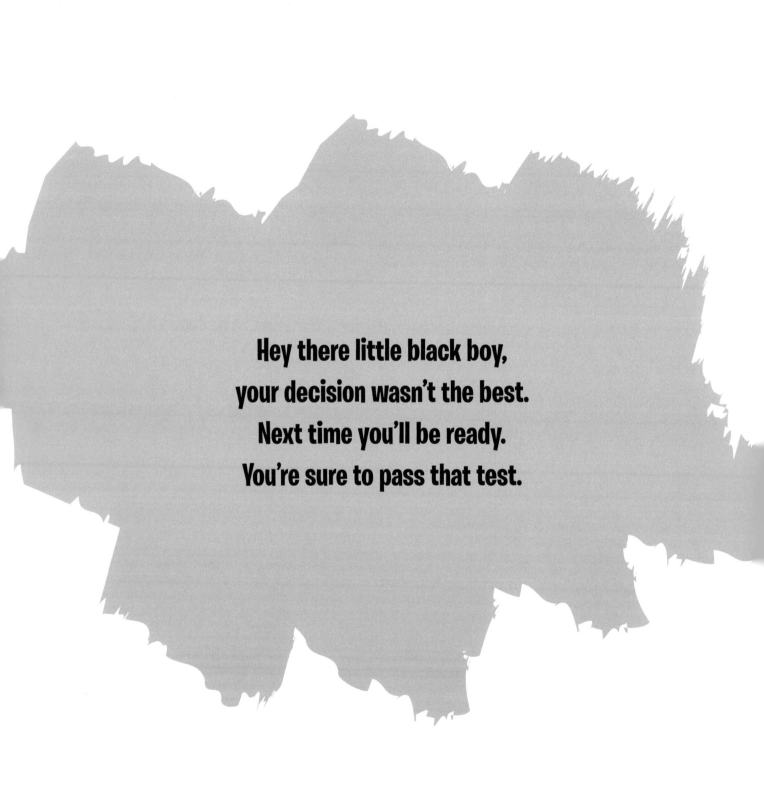

Hey there little black boy,
your decision wasn't the best.
Next time you'll be ready.
You're sure to pass that test.

Hey there
little black boy,
this time the
joke's on you.
When all you hear
is laughter,
you should just
laugh too!

Letter From the Author

I want to start out by saying thank you! Thank you for taking the time to read this book.

Thank you for bringing your beautiful child into the world.

Thank you for instilling love and support into your child's life.

This book is a passion project for me and really serves to meet a need that I have had even well into my adult life.

My parents loved us. I have a brother and a sister and we all received our parent's love in different ways.

Unfortunately, receiving love from a parent isn't always enough.

I have found that a huge portion of the love that I didn't receive wasn't supposed to come from my parents.

I grew up not knowing where that love was supposed to come from. I didn't have anyone to teach me to love myself.

To tell me that I was special, and magical, and wonderful, and talented, and perfectly imperfect. In my adult life,

I want to be that voice for so many children. I want children to know that they must love THEMSELVES.

That's where this book comes in.

This book is supposed to be a guide for parents to connect with their children.

To help them learn their feelings and figure out how to deal with them.

This book speaks to the hearts and souls of both the children this book targets and the parents that will read

this book to their children. We are all deserving of the love and magic that lie inside of us.

My hope is that this book will pave the way for showing each of us how to learn and love ourselves.

Happy reading!